Guide to

H I S T O R I C

Durango & Silverton

D1611330

Duane A. Smith

CORDILLERA PRESS, INC.
Publishers in the Rockies

Library of Congress Cataloging-in-Publication Data

Smith, Duane A.
    Guide to historic Durango & Silverton / Duane A. Smith. — 1st ed.
      p.   cm.
    ISBN: 0-917895-16-9: $4.95
    1. Durango (Colo.) — Description — Tours. 2. Silverton (Colo.) —
Description — Tours. 3. Historic sites — Colorado — Durango — Guide-books.
    4. Historic sites — Colorado — Silverton — Guide-books.
    5. Durango (Colo.) — History. 6. Silverton (Colo.) — History.
    I. Title. II. Title: Guide to historic Durango and Silverton.
    F784.D9S63   1988
    917.88'29 — dc 19   88-12298
                                                 CIP

Cover photographs of Silverton train departing Silverton and preparing to take on water at the Needleton tank by Ron Ruhoff, Evergreen, Colorado.
Interior photographs not otherwise credited by Glen Crandall, Durango, Colorado.

Cover design by Richard M. Kohen, Shadow Canyon Graphics, Evergreen, Colorado.
Typography and design by Shadow Canyon Graphics, Evergreen, Colorado.

First Edition
   2 3 4 5 6 7 8 9
Printed in the United States of America
ISBN: 0-917895-16-9

Cordillera Press, Inc., P.O. Box 3699, Evergreen, Colorado 80439   (303) 670-3010

Contents

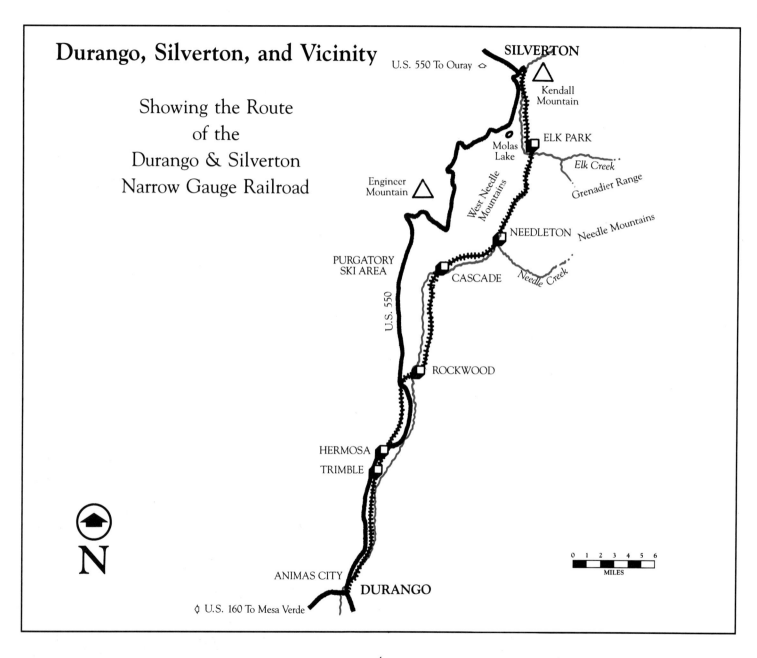

Durango, Silverton, and Vicinity

Showing the Route
of the
Durango & Silverton
Narrow Gauge Railroad

SILVERTON

U.S. 550 To Ouray

Kendall
Mountain

Molas
Lake

ELK PARK

Elk Creek

Grenadier Range

Engineer
Mountain

West Needle
Mountains

NEEDLETON

Needle Mountains

PURGATORY
SKI AREA

CASCADE

Needle Creek

U.S. 550

ROCKWOOD

HERMOSA
TRIMBLE

N

0 1 2 3 4 5 6
MILES

ANIMAS CITY

DURANGO

◊ U.S. 160 To Mesa Verde

Durango, Silverton, and Mining in the San Juans

Mining in the San Juan Mountains dates back to the 1760s when Juan Maria de Rivera and fellow Spanish explorers found precious metals amidst those rugged peaks. No mining industry developed, however. The area was remote, the Indians hostile, and the problems of ore production complex. Mining the San Juans would have to wait.

Nearly a century passed. Then in 1859, the Pike's Peak gold rush brought thousands of miners surging west to the Rocky Mountains where they founded communities such as Denver, Georgetown, Black Hawk and Central City. Some fifty-niners pushed across the Front Range of the Rockies, ascended the Arkansas River, and in 1860 found gold in California Gulch near the future site of Leadville. In the midst of the rush, Charles Baker led another group of intrepid prospectors into the remote San Juan country where they found gold in what became known as Baker's Park, the future site of Silverton. But again, deep snows, bitter cold, and hostile Ute Indians frustrated the mining of gold and, later, silver.

The news of gold in Baker's Park, however, could not be denied. Despite the obvious dangers, more and more prospectors braved the hazards in hope of finding instant wealth . . . if they survived. In the late 1860s many of these men, working from snowmelt to snowfall, then retreating for the winter, gradually opened the San Juans and paved the way for permanent settlement. In the Brunot Treaty of 1873 the Utes surrendered large areas of the San Juans and this further speeded settlement, although Ute reservation claims remained a point of contention. By the mid-1870s, Silverton had emerged as a rough mining camp, but the area still remained isolated and remote. Despite new toll roads built by various entrepreneurs, including the Russian-born Otto Mears, even then developing his reputation as the "Pathfinder of the San Juans," the limited transportation system continued to inhibit mining.

What changed the San Juans forever was the Denver & Rio Grande Railway, founded by General William Jackson Palmer, a Union cavalry officer during the Civil War, and the group of eastern and English investors he headed. In the early 1870s, Palmer's narrow gauge line built south from Denver, bent upon laying track all the way to Mexico City. The silver discoveries at Leadville, however, and the loss of vital Raton Pass to the Atchison, Topeka, and Santa Fe Railroad, caused the road to switch goals, wrest control of the strategic Royal Gorge from the Santa Fe, and lay track west into central Colorado. Not content with reaching Leadville, Palmer's line built south and west across the mountains to tap many other mining camps. By the early 1880s the Rio Grande's arrival in the San Juans gave new impetus to mining.

Wherever Palmer and his associates went, they launched other business ventures that could take advantage of the new railroad link. The San Juans were no exception. A loosely organized group known as the Durango Trust founded the town of Durango, purchased coal and hard-rock mines, and built a smelter to reduce ore to bullion.

Once the Rio Grande arrived in Durango, it turned its eyes north toward Silverton. Track layers put down rails through the forests, across the streams, and along the cliffs, building a line that was as spectacular as the mountains. The railroad not only spurred mining at Silverton and other towns, but also induced other railroads to tap more distant mining camps.

This guide provides a glimpse of the historic mining frontier as it unfolded in Durango and Silverton. As you visit here, please remember that your respect for the natural and historic environment as well as private property will ensure preservation of these historic areas for future visitors.

Stanley Dempsey
General Editor
Cordillera Press Historic Mining District Series

Above: In the early 1880s, the new city of Durango had a sparse, treeless look. The smelter belches smoke in the background. *William Henry Jackson photograph. Denver Public Library, Western History Department.* *Left:* Townspeople watch workers install the first cistern in downtown Durango about 1880. *Colorado Historical Society.*

Animas City and Durango: The Struggle for Survival

Mines, towns, and railroads were the three keys in developing the nineteenth-century San Juans. Mining came first, then communities grew to serve the miners, and finally, the Denver & Rio Grande Railway arrived to link the towns with the outside world and launch a new era of prosperity.

Durango was born in 1880 when the Denver & Rio Grande, headed by the energetic William Jackson Palmer, planned a line that would tap what appeared to be the profitable mines around Silverton. To reach Silverton, Palmer's men needed a good launching point. They soon learned that the curving valley of the Animas River, several thousand feet lower and a day's travel south of Silverton, held many attractions. Coal outcroppings surfaced in several places — coal needed by the railroad as well as the smelter the men hoped to construct. The valley offered easy access from all directions — a plus for future expansion. Abundant water, along with a longer growing season and milder climate than graced the mountains, would attract farmers and ranchers. Hot springs, mysterious Indian ruins, and grand scenery would lure visitors. All that would translate into sales, freight, passengers, and income for the Rio Grande.

The Animas River Valley had already drawn farmers, ranchers, and other settlers who raised the crops and cattle needed by

the miners. In the early 1870s, Animas City, a small village with a hopeful name, had sprung to life, snuggled between the Animas River and flat-topped Animas Mountain.

By 1879, the future looked bright for Animas City. Crops were good. Boosters hailed the riches in the mines to the west up Junction Creek as a "marvel." Developers had opened "mammoth" coal banks to the south. There was talk of becoming the county seat. Townspeople here in one of the nation's youngest cities cheered the nation's 103rd birthday with "pop-crackers," races, speeches, lemonade, music by the ladies with "organ accompaniment," and a "hop in the evening."

A couple of months later, the nation displayed its might in Animas City when troops marched in to guard the region from the Ute Indians after the killing of Nathan Meeker and others some miles distant at White River. The army garrisoned soldiers in Animas City until it established Fort Lewis a short distance away on the La Plata River.

Animas City also hoped to become the railroad center of the San Juans, but that brought problems. The Rio Grande demanded certain concessions, but the city haughtily refused to grant them. Then the railroad threatened to establish a rival com-

munity. Still, Animas City stood firm. The townspeople should have paid more attention to the Rio Grande. This was not a bluff, but a tactic Palmer's men had used many times before. Too late the Animas City town fathers realized that the future of their community, like so many of its counterparts, rested on gaining the railroad — on its terms.

When negotiations failed, the Rio Grande founded Durango. In December 1879, the *La Plata Miner*, published in Silverton, carried several items about the new, beautifully located "railroad town two miles below Animas City." In the Animas City column, the editors published one writer's prophetic observation that the new town "will knock the stuffing out of the present town, yet it will be a good thing for us all, and especially our San Juan neighbors."

In May 1880, the editor of Animas City's *Southwest* took time to poke fun at the rival community. "What the 'new town of Durango' is to be or not to be, God and The D&RG Railroad only know." But the editor laughed neither last nor best this time. The Rio Grande patented coal claims and located other land in anticipation of coming developments. In September, surveying began on the townsite. Sales jumped overnight, and by Christmastime nearly 2,500 people — many of them railroad workers wintering over until work resumed in the spring — had arrived.

Animas City's future died with Durango's birth, the high hopes gone to yesterday. The newspaper, bank, several businesses, and many residents packed up and journeyed south those fateful two miles to booming Durango. There was no time for tears, no time for regrets, no time to ponder the lessons of history.

Then in 1881, as soon as the weather permitted, the Rio Grande started to lay track. The rails and work trains reached Durango in July, but the official celebration, the "EVENTFUL DAY," did not take place until August 5. There was a parade, a baseball game (Durango 10-3 over Silverton), and a "grand hop" at the new smelter that evening. The gala celebration made almost everyone forget that the invited dignitaries had not arrived — a washout eighty miles from town had stopped their train. Undaunted, the festivities continued the next day and the speeches and welcome were hardly worse for the delay.

The Denver & Rio Grande had orchestrated the opening act. No longer a dream, Durango crowded along dusty streets that crisscrossed the sagebrush valley. Few trees graced the spare landscape, and across the river the new smelter belched smoke as it reduced silver ore to silver bullion. The railroad had arrived as promised, and mining towns like Silverton now awaited their own celebration as soon as the Rio Grande could build north. The future looked bright, but only the railroad could chart what that future would bring.

Left: General William Jackson Palmer, president of the Denver & Rio Grande Railway. *Colorado Historical Society. Below:* Looking north from the Durango smelter across the Animas River into Durango. Note the roundhouse and railroad yards just across the river. *Colorado Historical Society.*

Durango: Railroad Born, Destiny's Child

Durango, the "magic metropolis" as it pleased to call itself, began a planned community. The Durango Trust, handmaiden of the Denver & Rio Grande, believed firmly in town planning. The railroad's president, William Jackson Palmer, had followed this course many times, most notably in the founding of Colorado Springs.

In Durango, the business district would occupy the river bottom, while the residential area developed on the benches stepping eastward, crowned by a grand boulevard with a tree-lined parkway separating traffic. Homeowners would find stunning views of the mountains, and noise and dust from the commercial hub would not disturb either social hours or evening rest. The Durango Trust donated free lots to churches, gave a lot for city hall and another for a school, and even set aside land for two parks and one entire block for the county seat, which organizers optimistically hoped to seize from the small and declining mining camp of Parrott City.

Thanks to its railroad backing, Durango grew by leaps and bounds. The *Durango Record* conducted a business survey in March 1881, and found among the establishments, four hardware stores, five lumber companies, one bank, ten real estate firms, six hotels, twelve lawyers, three newspapers, twenty saloons, and one church. A grand total of 134 businesses were listed, a fact the editor thought amazing for a six-month-old town. The Durango Trust was pleased as well. In August, Trustee William A. Bell wrote an investor that "the Town of Durango is assuming the proportions of a city."

By the end of 1881, Durango displayed characteristics that charted its development for the next century: boosterism, a grow-or-die philosophy, real estate speculation, determination to become southwestern Colorado's queen city, and the aggressiveness to carry out its dreams.

In the ensuing years Durango lived up to its rapid start. Its smelter served an area stretching to Silverton and Red Mountain, sixty miles to the north, and northwest to Rico and Telluride once the Rio Grande Southern Railroad reached there in the early 1890s.

While no nearby gold and silver mines brightened Durango's days, local coal mines provided a less glamorous source of income, but, more important, fuel for home, smelter, and business. Local coal powered the dynamos which started generating electricity in 1887, making Durango one of the first cities in Colorado to adopt this new form of power and light. The *Durango Herald* of January 12, 1888, cheered its readers on by declaring that "the electric light is becoming popular and should be used in every business house and residence in the city."

By 1893, a trolley connected the Rio Grande depot with Animas City and had two cars clanging up and down Main Avenue. For the first time, up-to-date Durango was no longer simply a walking community, and suburbs soon stretched northward toward the older, now humbled Animas City.

A second railroad, the Rio Grande Southern, linked Durango via a wide, northwestward arc with farms in the Montezuma Valley, mines at Rico and Telluride, and eventually Ridgway. Otto Mears, the legendary "Pathfinder of the San Juans," built the Rio Grande Southern, backed largely by Denver & Rio Grande money. Mears' tracks merged with the larger line at both ends. Durango's transportation cup overflowed.

So did developments within the community, which emerged as the second largest town on Colorado's Western Slope — that nearly 40 percent of the state west of the Continental Divide. By 1900, 3,317 Durangoans lived within the city limits along the banks of the Animas River. They approved as the physical appearance rapidly changed, losing the "frontier town characteristics," as George Crofutt applauded in his 1885 *Grip-Sack Guide of Colorado*. It had become

Ox teams hauling a building down Main Street. This structure was mistakenly built on the Denver & Rio Grande right-of-way and had to be moved. *First National Bank.*

The Newman Block rises behind a Durango, Brookside & Animas City streetcar. *Center of Southwest Studies.*

a "resident center." A few years later Durango was hailed as a "church center" and as the "home of mining men and of wealth."

Even the disastrous fire of July 1, 1889, rushed along by a "terrific wind," which destroyed much of the business district and some thirty homes and three churches, could not stop Durangoans. Despite a generally uninsured loss of over $500,000 in goods and buildings, rebuilding started almost before the ashes cooled. Durangoans and their community rebounded quickly; the *Herald* of January 1, 1890, declared "nothing can possibly keep her back."

New Englander Estelle Camp, wife of banker Alfred P. Camp, might have complained about the scarcity of women when she arrived as a bride in 1883, but she need not have fretted. Eight years later serious discussion ensued about forming a Ladies Athletic Club. "The wives, mothers, sisters and daughters of Durango, should have a suitable building in which they can enjoy regularly such exercises as they most need for their physical development." While the club never came to pass, a scarcity of women no longer existed.

Estelle also worried about the two extremes of social life. On one hand there was the "cultured, well educated, traveled class," and on the other, the "wild and wooly followers of the mining and lumber camps and cattle ranges." Again she need not have fretted. Durango soon had all the trappings of Victorian middle class respectability. The women quickly smoothed the rough frontier edges, and churches, schools (even a high school), musicals, socials, dances, clubs, a library, fine homes, a hot springs resort (though nary an opera house) showed to one and all that here grew a genteel, refined community. "Our beautiful town is really attaining metropolitan proportions," cheered the *Durango Record* and its outspoken, feisty editor Caroline Romney as early as March 18, 1882.

For the men, there were lodge meetings to attend, fire companies to join, fishing and hunting expeditions to take, and a baseball team to support in leisure hours. They could also partake of commercial entertainment in two red-light districts. Despite protests by determined reformers, the

A trolley pauses at 9th and Main streets, dressed up for a holiday about 1900. *La Plata County Historical Society.*

A passenger train ready to leave the station at Durango. *Denver Public Library, Western History Department.*

The roundhouse at Durango, 1955. *Denver Public Library, Western History Department.*

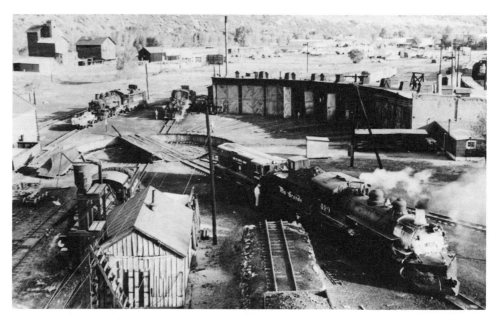

saloons, gambling halls, and prostitutes stayed — they were, after all, good for local business.

All the good times came to an end in the silver crash of 1893. Never had Durangoans seen such an economic crash and depression. Optimism disappeared, confidence waned. Charcoal kiln worker Frank Burke expressed a common feeling, if not common solution. "Times too hard. What I owe now I'll owe forever," he wrote in his suicide note.

For years Durangoans and other Americans suffered through the worst depression the country had yet endured. Not until the turn of the century would Durango spring back, although many decades would pass before the real boom and growth times came again. By then, the world and Durango had changed markedly and two generations of Durango men and women had marched off to world wars.

After World War II, Durango raced into the greatest boom of its history. Tourism, oil and gas exploration, and the uranium rush triggered unprecedented growth and prosperity. The town's population nearly doubled in twenty years to over 10,000 people by 1960. The move of Fort Lewis College into Durango generated additional economic, educational, and cultural sparks. Durango of the 1980s would have made its founders proud. It had become and remained the economic hub of southwestern Colorado; yet it had retained its nineteenth-century charm.

Durango in the early twentieth century, after the trees had grown. *Colorado Historical Society.*

Smelting City of the San Juans

No visitor should "miss the opportunity to inspect the massive works," the *Durango Herald* reported on August 5, 1881. The writer correctly forecast that the smelter under construction would "inevitably make Durango the main smelting city of the San Juans."

Backed by the Denver & Rio Grande Railway and managed by the experienced mining and smelting man, John Porter, the smelter "blew in" to an enviable start. By 1887, it processed over a million dollars worth of silver, lead, gold, and copper per year, the ninth largest output in Colorado. Porter steadily improved his works and succeeded in driving out local competition. Optimistically, Porter wrote on January 8, 1891, that "the outlook for the smelting business is splendid."

At its peak the smelter employed over 300 men, with a monthly payroll of $30,000. After the silver crash of 1893, the smelter eventually fell under the control of the gigantic, monopolistic American Smelting and Refining Company. Unfortunately, labor disputes followed the ownership change. In 1899 and again in 1903 the workers struck; the first strike spread throughout Colorado before a company victory.

As mining declined in the twentieth century, so did the smelter's importance. The *Durango Democrat* of November 15, 1912, observed that yesterday was pay day, and while the stores used to keep open late, they "seldom do now." But the plant's noisy, smoky, smelly presence lingered. Finally, on November 1, 1930, the smelter closed, a victim of the Great Depression.

The smelter reopened during World War II to process vanadium and "a military secret," which turned out to be uranium. The plant closed again in 1945, then reopened three years later to mill and concentrate uranium ore. Once again the old smelter proved to be a major force in Durango's economy as yet another mining rush overran western Colorado and spilled into the other four-corner states.

The Vanadium Corporation of America purchased the plant in 1953 and operated it until early 1963. Then, for the final time, the smelter closed and gradually the remaining buildings were torn down. Despite arguments to the contrary from local preservationists, the last smokestack and buildings were demolished in 1987 as part of a clean-up project to remove "hot" uranium tailings.

The Durango smelter sitting on a bench above the Animas River rapids in 1892, the year before the silver crash. *Strater Hotel.*

Denver & Rio Grande Depot

The railroad depot, erected in 1881-82, is one of Durango's oldest buildings. The "new depot is a beauty," crowed the *Durango Herald* of April 8, 1881. But the editor also advocated that accommodations be materially improved. He was dismayed by waiting rooms that were not lighted, heated, or opened to the public "more than half the time."

The town's love/hate relationship with the Rio Grande was typical of western communities. All towns wanted a railroad connection, but most found themselves dominated by this outside force when it did come. Competition among railroads lessened this effect, and before Durango's major railroad era came to an end, several lines had come to town. The Rio Grande Southern, a short spur line to the coal mine behind Perin's Peak, and, later, the so-called "red apple" line, a Rio Grande standard gauge branch to Farmington, provided other outlets, but no relief from the Rio Grande's dominance.

The depot was the southern end of the trolley line that ran north up Main Avenue to Animas City. First horse-drawn, then electrified in 1892, it operated for thirty years.

Denver & Rio Grande Depot.

General Palmer Hotel

This lot sat vacant until the turn of the century, when it became the site of a saloon, and furniture and grocery stores. Converted to the Savoy Hotel, it acquired steam heat and electric lights and eventually evolved into the General Palmer Hotel.

The area around the depot served primarily railroad patrons and south-end Durangoans. In 1883, the National Hotel stood on the block's west side, near the present parking lot. A cigar store, saloon, and some dwellings were interspersed with vacant lots.

By 1890, three guest hotels, a "boarding" hotel, a grocery store, and a barbershop constituted the business district of this end of Main Avenue. Twenty years later, it in-cluded seven saloons, a couple of restaurants, lodging houses, three hotels (the Palace was nearest to the depot), a grocery, a drugstore, and a second-hand store. A block south stood the Durango Iron Works.

Strater Hotel

A nineteenth-century community without a first-class hotel was poor, indeed. With the building of the Strater Hotel in 1887-88, Durango came of age. The *Idea*

General Palmer Hotel.

Durango Walking Tour

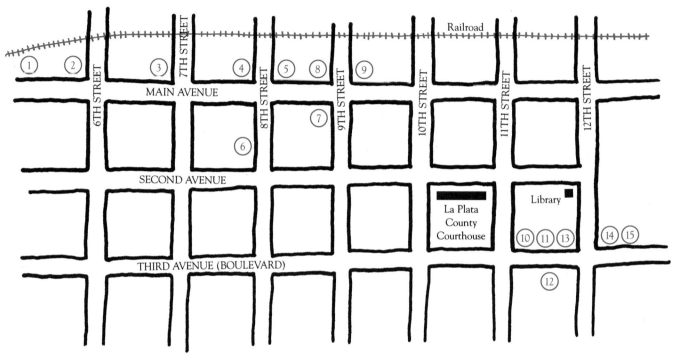

Key

1	Denver & Rio Grande Depot	9	First National Bank
2	General Palmer Hotel	10	Durango Christian Church / Methodist Church
3	Strater Hotel	11	Barrie House
4	Graden Building	12	Wigglesworth House
5	Newman Building	13	Presbyterian Church
6	Gallerie Marguerite	14	Wilson / Perkins House
7	Williams Block	15	Amy Home
8	Gardenswartz Building		

Strater Hotel.

proudly boasted on August 29, 1888, that the hotel presented "a decided metropolitan appearance to the eye." Durango's Strater could now challenge the best hotels of Denver, and visitors had no fear that they had left civilization behind when they came to this isolated corner of Colorado.

In 1892, a management dispute with a lessee spurred the hotel's owner, Henry Strater, to build a rival hostelry, the Columbian, directly south on the site of the old county offices. The crash of 1893 resulted in a merger of the two establishments (as they appear today) and eventually cost Strater the ownership of both.

The Strater retains its nineteenth-century charm for guests and other visitors. Its Diamond Circle Theater is the summer home of one of the country's finest melodramas.

Gallerie Marguerite

The Gallerie Marguerite and Goodman's, Inc. were, in earlier years, a mortuary run by one of Durango's oldest commercial families. George Goodman arrived in 1881 to join his brother Frank in a paint and wallpaper store which migrated to several different locations over the next century. Frank eventually left, but George stayed on and played a prominent role in the local volunteer fire companies and became the town's first salaried fire chief.

Second Avenue served as the buffer zone between the commercial and residential districts. A variety of small stores and homes, and since 1892 the La Plata County Courthouse, have lined the avenue. The library and the old high school grace its northern end today. John Elitch operated an Oyster House on Second Avenue in 1881-82, before he moved to Denver and found fame with his Elitch Gardens.

Gallerie Marguerite.

Graden Building

The present Graden Building sits on the location of the original Graden Mercantile Company. Thomas Graden came to Durango with the railroad as one of General Palmer's "boys."

In 1890, this corner included a Drug & Paint Store, the T. C. Graden General Store, and to the west, where the parking lot now lies, the T.C. Graden Wholesale Grocery. Offices occupied the second floor.

"One of the most popular men in Durango," Graden proved to be a successful entrepreneur. By 1893, he was head of the mercantile company, the Mancos Lumber Company, the Graden Flour Mill (now the site of the Red Lion Inn), and the "electric railroad." According to local legend, "Honest Tom" detested copper coins; any "pennies the cashier found in the till at night" were thrown out the window without further thought.

Graden Building.

Newman Block.

Newman Block

Southwestern Colorado druggist and mine investor Charles Newman built the Newman Block in 1892-93. Credited with being the first to "build a business in Durango," Newman sold his drug and stationery store in 1889. By then, he had made a small fortune from his Rico and Red Mountain mines and other investments.

The block opened just before the crash of 1893, and Durangoans cheered it as "truly palatial." The red sandstone was quarried near Dolores, and the building used steam heat and electric lights throughout. As one publication stated, "The Newman block is a credit to its owner . . . and is the finest business building so far erected in Durango."

Originally the home of the Smelter National Bank and a neighboring grocery store, it has accommodated numerous businesses over the years.

Gardenswartz Building

The Durango Trust advocated brick buildings within the heart of the business community for fire protection and a more distinguished appearance. Unfortunately, most businessmen ignored the recommendation and became victims of the fire that destroyed several downtown blocks on July 1, 1889.

The present Gardenswartz Building was one of the first brick buildings in the community, and it survived the fire. A variety of businesses and offices have occupied this site. For example, in 1886 a bookstore was on the corner, with the post office to the south. Business turnovers came frequently, and four years later the building housed a stationery and music store, a clothing store, and one that specialized in wallpaper and picture frames.

The Durango Trust showed a singular lack of imagination in naming its streets. This was originally the corner of G and 1st streets.

Gardenswartz Building.

Williams Block.

Williams Block

The Williams Block, constructed in 1890, has been the home of Parsons Drug Store ever since. Pioneer businessman and Jockey Club member John L. Parsons shared the first floor with a clothing store and a saddle and harness shop in 1893. The second floor contained offices; the third floor was added after the turn of the century.

The Durango Exchange, forerunner of the Chamber of Commerce, had offices here, as did various professional people. Banks, including the present Burns Bank (since 1910) have occupied the corner across the street (the Freeman Block) for over 90 years. The business district stretched two blocks north from here on Main Avenue; most of the original buildings burned in the 1889 fire.

Directly east of Parsons Drug Store, on Ninth Avenue, stood the Masonic Hall. Such fraternal organizations gave newcomers an entree into the community.

First National Bank

The corner of 9th and Main streets was the business heart of nineteenth-century Durango. The Bank of Durango, which later merged with the First National Bank, operated here from 1881 until it moved to its present location in 1981.

The bank survived the 1889 fire, only to burn in 1892, after which the present classic Victorian building was constructed. Bank president Alfred Camp weathered several economic storms to build the First National into Durango's strongest bank. At one time, it could claim to be the only national bank in an area larger than Rhode Island.

Federal rules and demands occasionally bedeviled banker Camp. In 1895, officials in Washington questioned the suitability of the bank's location. Camp replied, "Our situation is regarded as having the most central and desirable corner in Durango for business purposes." The bank stayed put. What might have raised the government's ire was the fact that the rest of the west side of the 900 block was part of the red-light district!

First National Bank.

Durango looking north from Smelter Mountain, 1982. *Author's Collection.*

Durango Christian Church/ Methodist Church

The church in the nineteenth-century western community represented a spiritual element that transcended the materialism of everyday life. It was a center for family worship and entertainment and a place where women could exercise leadership and find involvement denied them elsewhere by social custom.

The Methodists built their first church here in 1881 — "the finest yet completed in our infant city," hailed the *Herald* after the opening service on January 15, 1882. Rebuilt in 1890 after the fire the previous year, the church and the parsonage served that congregation until 1970. The Durango Christian Church purchased the building and continues services here.

Durango Christian Church.

When the Baptists and Episcopalians built their churches, Third Avenue had fulfilled the dream of its planners. Catholics constructed a hospital, school, convent, and church complex across the river in the North Durango addition and another church south of Sixth Street.

Barrie House

One of the charms of Third Avenue's architecture is that it represents everything from the homes of working men to the "mansions" of some of Durango's first families. Architectural styles cover the period from the 1880s to the 1920s.

Saloon owner James Barrie built this small home about 1885. It was later purchased by Robert Sloan, one of General Palmer's "boys" and the long-time president of the Graden Mercantile Company.

Originally constructed of wood, the house has been slightly altered over the years, both inside and out. Durango has been fortunate, however, in that neither of its historic districts, Main Avenue and Third Avenue, has suffered seriously from fires or architectural changes. At their leisure, visitors may get the feel for an era that is now gone. If time permits, a walk down the entire length of both Third and Main avenues gives a glimpse of a wide variety of architectural styles.

Barrie House.

Wigglesworth House.

Wigglesworth House

Built in 1882-83, this house eventually became the Wigglesworth home. The railroad career of Thomas Wigglesworth, the family patriarch, dated back to the Civil War. He ran the 1879-80 survey of the Rio Grande route to Silverton and worked as chief engineer and surveyor for the Durango-to-Rico portion of Otto Mears's Rio Grande Southern Railroad.

In 1901, Wigglesworth located and built the Boston Coal & Fuel Railroad to the company's coal mine on the west side of Perin's Peak. Constructed by Navajos, the line operated until the mine closed in 1926.

Mears again employed Wigglesworth to survey and construct the extension of his Silverton Northern from Eureka to Animas Forks in 1904. No other individual had a longer career in the early history of San Juan railroading than "Wig," as he was often called.

Presbyterian Church

This 1890 Presbyterian Church replaced the one destroyed in the great 1889 fire. The Presbyterians organized a church in Animas City in 1877 (closed in 1887) and in Durango in December 1881. Within six months, they had completed their building on this site. The manse next door was built in 1903.

The Durango Trust's offer of free lots to churches helped to make the boulevard the primary church street as well as the most prestigious residential area. Churches, schools, homes, a courthouse, and a city hall all helped to promote sales and create the settled, refined image that was so desirable.

The Trust had also planned a tree-lined parkway, but it took the Ladies' Improve-

An engine of the Boston Coal & Fuel Company parked on a track in Durango. The line ran to a coal mine near Perin's Peak, west of town. *Author's Collection.*

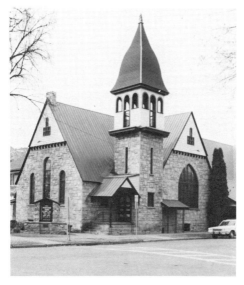

Presbyterian Church.

ment Society to turn that idea into reality in the 1890s and afterward. One of the two parks included in the original town plat was located where the Mason School grounds are today.

Wilson/Perkins House

This beautiful example of Queen Anne architecture was built in 1892. This style, popular from the 1870s into the 1890s, was typically elaborate, with porches, bay windows, an irregular floor plan, and unusual building materials. Although this particular design lost popularity in the East about 1890, it remained a favorite in Colorado well into the decade.

This house, built by Adair Wilson, a Durango lawyer, and his wife Margaret, went through several owners until it was

Wilson/Perkins House.

Amy House.

smelter changed ownership, but the home remained as a tribute to an era. "To look down upon the residences, trees, and green grass lawns from one of the many hills that surround Durango is a sight never to be forgotten for grandeur."

While in Durango, be sure to visit the La Plata County Museum, operated by the La Plata County Historical Society. Located at 3065 West Second Avenue, the museum, which was once the Animas City School, offers a variety of exhibits ranging from the early Anasazi culture to modern ranching. The museum is open from approximately Memorial Day through Labor Day. There is a minimal admission charge. Further information can be obtained by calling (303) 259-2402.

purchased by insurance and real estate agent Clayton Perkins in 1905. His family finally sold it in 1955. A carriage house was originally located on the rear of the lot; it was converted to apartments in 1930-31.

Combined with the neighboring Amy house, the Wilson residence gave the north end of Third Avenue a touch of class that rivaled any nearby community. No better examples of Durango's late nineteenth-century aspirations of greatness remain than these two homes.

Amy House

This 1888 mansion, now the Hood Mortuary, was early Durango's finest — the crown jewel of the boulevard (Third Avenue). Built by Ernest Amy, whose father was president of the smelting company, it cost nearly $50,000. The story is that it was intended to lure Amy's wife west from New York City. Other contemporary Durango homes cost between $1,000 and $2,500.

The Durango newspapers described it as among the "finest in the state," furnished "in elegant taste, and heated and lighted as a New York City mansion." Visitors were shown the Amy home "as soon as possible" to prove to them "that Durango is no mushroom city."

Amy and his family left town when the

Durango Driving Tours

Driving tours from Durango offer a variety of tempting subjects. Going east on 8th Street to 8th Avenue, then left up the hill brings you to Fort Lewis College. Once called Reservoir Hill because of the city reservoir located here, it was also the site of the famous gunfight between rustlers from Durango and Farmington in April 1881, the city's first airfield, a Civilian Conservation Corps camp, and, since 1956, the college.

Following U.S. 160 east to the Ignacio turnoff, State Highway 172 takes you to the Southern Ute Reservation and the tribal headquarters. Ignacio, a tri-ethnic community named for a famous Southern Ute leader, is a center for ranching and farming.

U.S. 160 west leads first to the Wildcat Canyon turnoff (County Road 141), the old route of the Rio Grande Southern Railroad. Up this road 1.8 miles once sat the coal camp of Porter, which did not outlive the end of mining in 1908. Little remains of it except some faint evidence of coal mining.

Farther west on U.S. 160 is Hesperus, a coal mining center dating from 1894. Some mining is still done in the area. A side trip south on Colorado 140 for 4.8 miles brings you to the site of the old Fort Lewis military post (1880-1891). It evolved into an Indian school, then to a high school, and finally to a junior college before becoming an agricultural research center. A few buildings remain from the military period.

A short distance beyond Hesperus (west on U.S. 160), County Road 124 leads north into La Plata Canyon. At the mouth of the canyon, the small settlement of May Day serviced nearby mines, including the May Day. A spur line of the Rio Grande Southern reached here. In a meadow slightly southwest of May Day was Parrott City, the first settlement (1873) in this part of Colorado and, for five years, the La Plata County seat. Parrott City was named for the San Francisco banking family which underwrote the early prospecting and mining of the district. Its agent, John Moss, led the party which established the camp and started permanent mining.

Farther up the beautiful canyon, a few homes remain from the little 1880s mining camp of La Plata. Isolated from the major San Juan mining and most of the state, the La Plata Mountains have never been a major mining area, but some mining, mostly for silver and gold, has continued off and on for over 100 years.

A return to U.S. 160 and a turn west will eventually lead you to Mesa Verde National Park. The cliff dwellings and mesa-top sites of the Anasazi are some of the most spectacular and best preserved in the Southwest. The Anasazi departed at the end of the thirteenth century, leaving behind villages, relics, and enduring mysteries about their culture and themselves. All this land was once theirs; numerous ancient sites underlie La Plata and Montezuma counties.

The very ambitious may want to take a grand circle trip which follows the route of Otto Mears' Rio Grande Southern Railroad much of the way: West from Durango on U.S. 160 to Mancos; northwest on Colorado 184 to Dolores (the section of Colorado 184 between Mancos and Dolores is designated the Dominguez-Escalante Highway in honor of two Franciscan priests who skirted the western San Juans on a 1776 expedition seeking a route from Santa Fe to California); then northeast up the spectacular Dolores River Canyon to Rico and over Lizard Head Pass to Telluride; and finally over Dallas Divide on Colorado 62 to Ridgway, where the Rio Grande Southern connected with the Denver & Rio Grande's Ouray branch. To complete the circle, return south to Durango on U.S. 550 via Ouray, "the Switzerland of America," rugged Red Mountain Pass, and Silverton. Molas Lake just south of Silverton offers a wonderful view of the San Juans.

All mountain roads require special caution. Please drive safely and sensibly.

A passenger train rounding the cliffs above the Animas River north of Rockwood. *Denver Public Library, Western History Department.*

Rails to Silverton

In late 1879, the world looked brighter than ever before to isolated, land-locked Silverton ensconced in Baker's Park. Denver & Rio Grande surveyors were at work in Animas Canyon, and the iron horse seemed almost at hand.

The editor of the *La Plata Miner* could not restrain himself. He predicted the beginning of a boom that "would not cease growing for a hundred years to come." In more restrained moments, he informed readers what the railroad would mean for the community and for mining. Among the benefits would be uninterrupted, year-long communication, greatly reduced and uniform freight rates, lower mining costs, the ability to ship low-grade ore, and possibly the construction of extensive smelting works. "In fact," he wrote, "it is impossible to estimate the great advantage in every way the completion of this road will be to our camp."

But such optimism completely masked the difficulties involved. Surveyors had to be let down canyon walls by rope, the roadbed blasted from solid rock, and numerous bridges built. Getting from Durango to Silverton was a major engineering challenge, so much so in fact, that the branch was later recognized as a National Historic Civil Engineering Landmark.

Throughout 1880, Silverton watched and waited. Expectations and delays caused dismay as the "plucky road" suffered one problem after another building to the San Juans. Silverton quickly learned that the railroad would be a mixed blessing. The local Greene smelter was purchased, dismantled, and shipped south to be erected as an economic bulwark for Silverton's new rival, Durango. Then, in August 1881, came complaints, echoed in the *La Plata Miner*, that William Jackson Palmer and his "outfit of skinners" had delayed building to "make Silverton valueless" so that they could buy up mines at "5% of their real value." No one had to look further than Animas City or other such towns to understand the railroad's power. Still, the editor and his readers knew they had no choice but to wait for rails and the economic benefits sure to come with the Silverton extension.

In fact, once the Rio Grande reached Durango in the summer of 1881, Palmer and his colleagues lost no time in building toward Silverton. They got as far as Rockwood, seventeen miles north, before winter closed in and ended track laying for the season.

Once spring returned, the Rio Grande braced itself for its most difficult construction project — the "high line" — a narrow shelf that had to be blasted out of the granite cliffs north of Rockwood. For one glorious season, that little camp enjoyed a boom as the marshalling point for the project. Five hundred men bent their backs in the cool mountain air. Silverton could hardly wait, and wondered if the railroad could not lay track a little faster. Down went the rails, and on Tuesday evening, June 27, 1882, Baker's Park heard that wonderful echo of an engine whistle. Two weeks later, the first train pulled into Silverton, forty-five mountainous miles and five hours and twenty minutes out of Durango.

"So far," said the *La Plata Miner* on July 15, "all that can be done by the outside world has been done, for by this medium it has been opened to us — what now remains is for us to do — to commence to make ourselves and make good our statements." All the benefits of modern transportation were now Silverton's.

But the bad came with the good. That same July, the newspaper reported two lady fortune-tellers "perambulating" on the streets along with occasional beggars of the "professional class." "Silverton heretofore had been exempt of these parasites," railed the editor. But with the advent of the railroad, he cautioned, the town could expect to be inflicted with increasing numbers of them.

Although Silverton enjoyed the benefits

of modern rail service, mother nature could still deal a mean hand. In the winter of 1883-84, snow blocked the tracks for 73 days, and in October 1911, the "flood of the century" washed out bridges and rails and stopped operations for nine weeks. In 1927 and again in 1932 Silverton was snow-locked for more than a month when avalanches closed the line. The railroad had penetrated, but not conquered, the San Juans.

Despite such inconveniences, the economy of Silverton was tied to the railroad. Long after many other Denver & Rio Grande branches had been pushed into oblivion by declining mining operations and the coming of the automobile, the Durango-Silverton run retained its importance as a reliable transportation route through the mountainous terrain separating the two communities.

By the end of World War II, snowplows kept what became U.S. 550 open over Coalbank Pass and Molas Divide through the winter and the railroad's importance finally waned. The 1950s saw the Denver & Rio Grande rid itself of most of its narrow gauge branches, but despite several attempts to do so, it never received permission from the Public Utilities Commission to abandon the Silverton branch. In part, opposition to abandonment came from a growing number of rail fans and tourists who arrived

A locomotive equipped with a wedge plow waiting in the Durango yards. *Denver Public Library, Western History Department.*

in increasing numbers to ride what was soon the last regularly scheduled narrow gauge passenger run in the country.

By 1962, the Rio Grande gave in to this show of support and launched a development campaign — however begrudgingly — to preserve and operate the line as a tourist railroad. Under the National Historic Preservation Act, the Durango-Silverton branch was declared a National Historic Landmark in 1967. As ridership increased, the railroad provided the scenes for a number of movies, including the western classic "Butch Cassidy and the Sundance Kid."

By the late 1970s, the Rio Grande was again looking to divest itself of the narrow gauge, and in 1981, it sold the line to the Durango & Silverton Narrow Gauge Railroad Company, which was committed to preserving this spectacular railroad legacy. Durango & Silverton President Charles E. Bradshaw, Jr. has declared that "there will never be a diesel locomotive run on Durango & Silverton Narrow Gauge tracks." The railroad continues to expand service to meet ever increasing ridership demands. Today, more than 170,000 passengers a year ride "the train to yesterday" and are provided a glimpse of what times were like in the heady days of Colorado's great mining boom.

Top, right: Dapper train passengers posing with the conductor at Durango, circa 1900. *Colorado Historical Society. Bottom, right:* Waiting for the train — the Durango station. *Colorado Historical Society.*

A work train stopped between Durango and Silverton sometime in the 1880s. *Flora Downtain.*

A double-headed Rio Grande passenger train curving around the mountains on the high-line north of Rockwood. The Animas River lies below. *William Henry Jackson photograph. Colorado Historical Society.*

A locomotive belching smoke as it runs to break through a snowslide near Silverton. *Colorado Historical Society.*

Digging out a snowslide near Silverton. *Colorado Historical Society.*

A rotary plow clearing track at Durango about 1900. *Colorado Historical Society.*

Riding the Durango & Silverton Narrow Gauge Railroad

The Durango & Silverton operates from about May 1 through October 30. Round-trip rates for the 90-mile ride are $37.15 for adults and $18.65 for children ages 5 through 11. Children under 5 ride free providing they do not occupy a seat. Trains leave Durango in the morning and schedules provide ample time in Silverton for lunch and shopping. During the peak summer season, four trains daily operate on the line. Because of the numerous schedules, it is very important to make reservations well in advance and then confirm boarding and departure times with the depot in Durango. The depot is located at 479 Main Avenue and the reservation number is (303) 247-2733. Tickets must be picked up by 6:00 p.m. the evening before the trip. Firearms, pets, and alcoholic beverages are not permitted on the trains. Several private cars are available for group charters and a special coach is equipped with wheelchair lifts. It really is a spectacular adventure!

Colorado Mountain Club members riding atop a caboose near Needleton on the club's 1920 outing. *Carl Blaurock.*

Backpacking in the San Juans

Riding the Silverton train adds excitement to a backpacking trip into the Needle Mountains or their northern neighbor, the rugged Grenadier Range, from stops at Needleton and Elk Park. Needleton is frequently used as a starting point by backpackers intent on climbing the 14,000-foot peaks of Sunlight, Windom, and Eolus, while Elk Park and the Elk Creek trail provide access to the less-traveled slopes of Arrow, Vestal, and Storm King peaks. The most comprehensive guide to backpacking and mountaineering in the San Juans is *The San Juan Mountains, A Climbing and Hiking Guide* by Robert F. Rosebrough.

Durango & Silverton policies and schedules for accommodating hikers, backpackers, and climbers have varied over the years. It is highly recommended that you call the main reservation number, (303) 247-2733, well in advance of your trip to ascertain schedules. No pets or firearms are permitted on the trains and backpacks are usually stored in the baggage car for the trip.

Silverton as it looked about 1900. *Denver Public Library, Western History Department.*

Silverton: Queen of the Silver Land

Buried deep in the heart of the San Juans, Silverton stood unbowed, a pugnacious eight years old, when the Denver & Rio Grande arrived. A survivor in the urban struggle for dominance on the Colorado mining frontier, this camp already had faced its share of ups and downs.

With aggressive leadership, a prime location in a beautiful mountain-ringed valley and a little luck, Silverton soon dominated its nearby rivals of Howardsville, Eureka, and Animas Forks. They, and a couple of even smaller hamlets, fell protesting into Silverton's economic orbit.

Within two years of its birth, Silverton claimed a newspaper, two reduction works, sawmills, a growing business district, and was the San Juan County seat. The community appeared well on its way to matching the destiny its boosters dreamed for it.

Only two problems stood in the way. One proved seasonal, with winter's approach, mining nearly stopped and most people migrated to lower, warmer climates. Freighter Ben Marsh expressed a common sentiment when writing his wife. "I think times will grow better here every year for several years to come. If the season were only longer and warmer it would be much better." The climate could never be overcome, yet the impact could be lessened with growth and improved transportation.

Alfred Camp, future husband of Estelle, put his finger clearly on the other problem. This would-be miner wrote in his 1875 journal: "One feels as if he is eventually (or so it seems) shut off from the rest of the world as there seems no way out."

Long, narrow, steep, rocky trails did lead to the outside. Time consuming and seasonal, they raised freighting costs and local tempers.

Silverton residents possessed an extra dose of optimism and confidence just to live in Baker's Park. No Colorado mining region was more isolated. And other districts kept grabbing publicity and tapping investors' pocketbooks with an ease that never blessed San Juaners' efforts.

They certainly faced problems and the railroad offered the elixir. Until the moment it arrived, residents made the best of the situation, busily setting about to create a community which resembled its older, more settled relatives back east. That way they could encourage investors and families to come and show one and all that Silverton was the "Queen of the Silver Land," as they grandiosely described their camp. The 1880 census credited "the Queen" with a population of 264.

While it might not have enough residents yet to qualify for anything but mining camp status, Silverton strove mightily to emulate

Victorian urban society. Lodges and clubs quickly took root. In mining's transitory world, being a member of the Masons, for example, gave a newcomer the key to open doors in the district's business and mining circles. The Masons and the Knights of Labor also both sponsored social events.

Literary Society members listened to poems, heard a "spirited debate" on the woman's suffrage question, and a paper in 1882 on the "pioneering life" of 1874. Such meetings were carefully reported in the newspaper (they helped give the proper community image) and it proved especially gratifying to discuss the long gone "pioneering days" and Silverton's founders. That certainly conveyed the right impression of rapid progress!

Ministers came seeking a flock, almost as soon as the prospector staked his claim. Nothing furnished a better image than the establishment of a congregation and the building of a church. The *La Plata Miner* proudly noted the debt-free dedication of the First Congregational Church in July 1881, "thanks to the liberal subscriptions of our citizens." Those farsighted people could congratulate themselves on having a church building which would be an "ornament to any town."

The Silverton Jockey Club and the baseball team gave the sporting crowd out-

The Salvation Army String Band at Silverton. *Denver Public Library, Western History Department.*

lets. They were especially active around holidays such as the "glorious fourth." Community pride suffered a blow and the betting crowd's purse shrunk when the local nine lost to Durango, 11-7, after "splendid playing" in 1881. That defeat, however, did not permanently dampen the celebration.

Silverton felt secure enough by the 1880s to poke fun at rivals and loved twisting the knife into upstart Durango. After a morning gunfight in Durango between two rustling gangs, the *Miner* gloated: "Deadly Durango

and fatal Farmington, twin sisters of the knife and bullet, is it not time ye were taking a rest?"

Just before the railroad appeared in 1882, a mining exchange opened with a permanent exhibition of San Juan ores. And the iron horse's arrival let Silverton pat itself on the back as the "most substantial and promising town in Southern Colorado."

The Rio Grande provided Silverton the final advantage over all its mountain neighbors. By 1885, the population topped 1,000

people, and the business district reflected that growth. Silverton had become the transportation hub, and the business, social, and mining center of the San Juan district. No longer an isolated mining camp, it had evolved almost overnight into a thriving mining town.

It would not be an unmixed blessing. The outside world came crashing in with fads, industrialization, corporate dominance, tourism, and changes. Still Silverton desired more and eventually three short narrow gauge lines crept further out of town to tap mines at Red Mountain, Gladstone, and Animas Forks. Also, two other worthy San Juan rivals eventually gained railroad connections, Ouray and Telluride. Silverton would not have all the advantages to herself.

In the end, though, the Denver & Rio Grande allowed Silverton to fulfill its dreams. Since 1882 the railroad has been a vital factor in the town's economic life.

Silverton and San Juan County's great mining days came slightly later than other areas in Colorado. Production averaged nearly $2 million a year in gold, silver, copper, lead, and zinc, during the first two decades of the twentieth century. A gradual decline followed, but mining never stopped, and the county remains one of the state's major gold producers.

Silverton evolved from strictly a mining town into one which relies on mining and tourism for its livelihood. Improved roads, cars, and trucks doomed the Rio Grande's passenger and freight hauling business until tourists discovered the scenic and historic wonders of the trip. That discovery gave new life to the communities on both ends of the line and, for Silverton, provided a summer bonanza.

All-weather highways meant that miners no longer had to live here — they could commute, and did, from as far away as Durango and Montrose. The business district declined, however, and now only in the summer months does it resemble its ancestor of a century ago. Meantime, Silverton, one of the few remaining Colorado mining towns, hangs onto its heritage, even as it evolves into its second century.

Miners and mules at the North Star Mine on King Solomon Mountain. This was a typical small mining operation of the 1880s. *Flora Downtain.*

This nine-piece band posed for the photographer — and posterity — just before they marched in a parade in Silverton, 1881. *Denver Public Library, Western History Department.*

Downtown Silverton in the 1880s. *Colorado Historical Society.*

"Batter Up!" Playing baseball at the Silverton School in 1884. *Denver Public Library, Western History Department.*

The *San Juan Herald* was one of Silverton's early newspapers. *Center of Southwest Studies.*

Fourth of July at Silverton. *Colorado Historical Society.*

Silverton Walking Tour

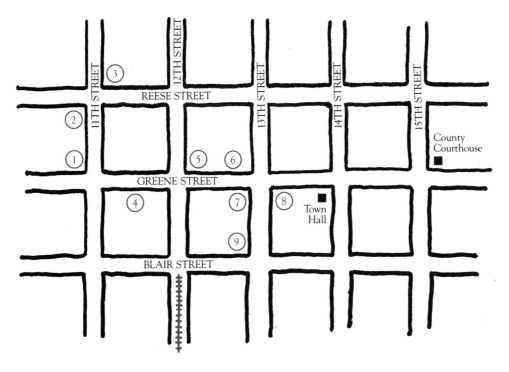

Key

1. Miners' Union Hall
2. Congregational / United Church of Christ
3. Silverton Library
4. Livery
5. Grand Imperial Hotel
6. *Silverton Standard & the Miner* Building
7. French Bakery and Teller House
8. Pickle Barrel
9. Swanson's Market

Miners' Union Hall

The Miners' Union Hall, constructed in 1901, represented a victory for the miners, who finally achieved union representation in this district after a long struggle. Until the 1890s, they had persisted in the hope that they could become owners upon the discovery of a promising claim. That hope had been dashed by large companies.

Miners had become day laborers, and the grim reality of their plight brought the union onto the scene. Neither the owners nor many other Americans esteemed unions very highly because they trailed a generation-old reputation for violence. From 1901 through 1904, the San Juans, and much of the rest of Colorado, witnessed the struggle between management and the Western Federation of Miners. The union eventually lost out after bitter fights.

The second floor of this building served as a community dance hall, and the main floor has housed a funeral parlor and a furniture store.

Congregational/United Church of Christ

Churches came early to Silverton, as they did to many Colorado mining communities. Itinerant preachers brought the first messages. The Reverend Joseph Pickett visited Silverton in June 1878, and held a Congregational service in the school house. A

Miners' Union Hall.

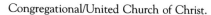

Congregational/United Church of Christ.

fierce snowstorm did not deter the dozen people who attended and became the core of a Sunday School and this church.

By the first week of July, Pickett was pleased to see nearly every child in town in the Sunday School. Even the "gamblers of the Jockey Club" donated $53 to purchase a library. Pickett, who enjoyed a brisk walk and retreat in the nearby mountains, did not remain permanently but went on to carry his message to other camps.

The cornerstone of the current building was laid in August 1880; the steeple was added in 1885. The oldest Congregational church in Colorado still holding services, it is now the United Church of Christ.

Silverton Library

Andrew Carnegie's steel mills made him a multimillionaire. Unlike many nineteenth-century financiers, he believed he should return part of his wealth to the American people. This he did by funding libraries.

Both Durango and Silverton benefitted from Carnegie's generosity. Silverton's library was built in 1906 at a cost of $12,000. It remains one of the best existing examples of Carnegie's original plans. The *Silverton Weekly Miner,* June 9, 1906, reported, "The building will be furnished in hardwood, as to floors, bookcases and furniture. The walls

Silverton Library.

to pay the license fee, livery stables did not attract attention from the city fathers or the newspaper columns. The coming of the horseless carriage doomed them, and by the 1920s, they had disappeared into history.

This building ("livery and transfer, coal and lime") was constructed in the mid-1890s by the Bowman family, which ultimately made its fortune with biscuits and the National Biscuit Company. It was one of Silverton's finest liveries.

Livery.

Grand Imperial Hotel.

and ceiling will be frescoed and the rooms lighted by beautiful electroleers."

A tour of the library will reveal that most of these furnishings are still in place. Like a school and a church, a library signified permanence and middle-class values. Earlier reading rooms and lending libraries had led in that direction, but the new library proved that Silverton had actually achieved its goal.

Livery

The livery stable, or the livery and feed stable, was an essential part of every mining town and many of the camps, although it was sometimes taken for granted. Where else could one rent a horse and buggy to court his best girl, find out the latest gossip, or pass some time with congenial friends?

Unless they became a nuisance because of the operator's carelessness or his failure

Grand Imperial Hotel

At each end of the Rio Grande's line, the traveler could find an excellent hotel. The Grand Hotel, now the Grand Imperial,

opened in 1883. It was built by Englishman W.S. Thomson, who, said the *San Juan Herald*, "became convinced that Silverton is the best town in southern Colorado." He also had interests in the local Martha Rose Smelter.

The first floor originally housed four businesses: two hardware stores, a dry goods business, and a gents' clothing store. Offices for lawyers, the phone company, and the county occupied the second floor; 38 rooms served guests.

The Grand was a prized feature of Silverton; the "most prosperous and promising camp in the entire San Juans" could ask for little more prestige than it provided. Over the years it has had a variety of owners, but has always remained a hotel. Businesses have come and gone on its first floor, one of the most famous being the Hub Saloon.

Silverton Standard and the Miner Building

The *Silverton Standard and the Miner*, a merger of earlier newspapers, is the oldest newspaper and continuous business on Colorado's Western Slope. The *La Plata Miner* began publishing in 1875.

Every mining town wanted a newspaper. In the war to advance itself and attract settlers and investors, a town needed a friendly press on which to call. The local newspaper avidly promoted, defended, and advertised its own town, while attacking rivals with a vengeance. In this era of personal journalism, the paper's editor defended the "true faith" of his political views, served as a community gadfly and social reporter, and tried to survive in a very competitive world.

Thirteen newspapers were born, merged, died, or moved from Silverton during the 1880s. The *Standard,* which started up in 1889, proved to be the survivor of the group. This building, one of the earliest that remains in town, dates from 1876-77.

French Bakery and Teller House

Brewery owner Charles Fischer constructed this building, which has evolved through a series of businesses that included the Teller House (rooming house), a saloon, a bakery, a grocery store, and now the French Bakery and Teller House. Each was important to Silverton's economy and demonstrated the attraction of a mining town to business.

The French Bakery, originally founded

Silverton Standard and the Miner Building.

French Bakery and Teller House.

about eighty years ago on Blair Street, was one of the few legitimate businesses in the red-light district. It moved to this site in 1916 and then became a grocery store under various names.

Silverton played its role as an immigrants' "melting pot." Many of the community's businessmen and miners came from Eastern Europe, a reflection of the wave of emigrants from that region after the turn of the century. August Maffey and Joe Machetto built the French Bakery on land they purchased from Domenica Dallavalle. Among their early patrons were the girls of Blair Street.

Pickle Barrel

Erected in 1880, the building now occupied by the Pickle Barrel originally housed Sherwin & Houghton, general merchants. Fred Sherwin was elected mayor in 1880 and bought out Peter Houghton in 1883. One of five similar stores, it faced keen competition, including two drug stores, a hardware store, a bakery, and two meat markets. A thriving mining town, as Silverton was, attracted a host of other businesses that same year, among them barbers, blacksmiths, boot and shoe stores, jewelers, newsdealers, and restaurants.

The *Denver Tribune,* September 21, 1881, stated that the "honest and public spirited" Silverton merchants enjoyed a "first class reputation at home and abroad." Perhaps no town in Colorado boasted a "more reliable and enterprising class of businessmen."

A continuing walk up Greene Street reveals the town hall on the next corner. It

Pickle Barrel.

San Juan County Courthouse.

parlor houses; in May 1906, there were 64. Because Silverton had ordinances against prostitution, the girls paid $384 in fines that May, a somewhat novel, but not unusual, way to ease a mining community's tax burden.

Swanson's Market.

Town Hall.

was built in 1908-09 at a cost of $14,550. A block farther is the San Juan County Courthouse, constructed in 1907. Next to it stands the 1902 jail, now the San Juan County Historical Society Museum.

Swanson's Market

The building housing Swanson's Market, dating from 1902, was originally the Tyrolean, and then the Minolla, Saloon. Before them, a small crib, part of the Blair Street red-light district, occupied the lot. Later converted into a boarding and rooming house, it became a grocery store in 1941. Swanson's Market is Silverton's oldest continuously operated family business.

Blair Street, the heart of Silverton's red-light district, offered dance halls, gambling rooms, saloons, and bordellos. It was an essential part of the town's business district and provided a needed entertainment center for the masculine world of San Juan mining.

The Police Magistrate's report of July 1904 listed 54 prostitutes in the cribs and

Silverton Driving Tours

Nestled in the heart of the San Juans, Silverton was surrounded by satellite communities which were part of its economic orbit. Silverton, fiercely protective of its interests in these communities, guarded against intrusion by outside rivals such as Ouray. All the small camps are gone today, but their locations are accessible and some of the surrounding smelter and mine sites can be seen from the road. Remember that much of what you see is private property and that *old mines are very dangerous.*

At the north end of Greene Street, the road forks and becomes County Road 110. A turn to the right (east) first takes you past the new Sunnyside Mill, then to Howardsville and beyond. The first San Juan County seat and once the oldest and largest county settlement, Howardsville sits on the west end of Stony Pass, the main route into this area. Once it lost the county seat to rival Silverton, Howardsville found its days of glory numbered. It continued to serve miners in the area, however, and the *San Juan Herald* of July 6, 1882, called it a "busy and prosperous town."

One and one-half miles beyond Howardsville, only one house remains at Middleton, a camp that dated from 1880. Despite a prediction that it would take its place "among the foremost of the San Juan," it never came close to deserving so much optimism.

Eureka, with its huge Sunnyside mill ruins, got off to a slow start but hit full stride after the turn of the century, when the Sunnyside emerged as one of the region's great mines. In 1896, when the camp became the terminus of Otto Mears' Silverton Northern Railroad, Eureka's fortunes soared. New residences, businesses, and a school soon testified to that.

Mears, a pioneer road and railroad builder whose toll roads crisscrossed the San Juans, began construction of his Silverton Northern in 1896, intending to take it all the way to Lake City. The rails reached Eureka easily enough (thirty minutes on the uphill pull, twenty-seven minutes downhill), but soon fell victim to financial difficulties and the problems of continuing up the steep canyon. In 1904, the tracks finally reached Animas Forks at a cost of about $27,000 per mile. For all the effort and expense, however, the line never proved to be a profitable addition, nor did the Silverton Northern ever reach Lake City.

The road beyond Eureka is best suited for four-wheel drive vehicles. Animas Forks, one of the San Juans' highest settlements (11,100 feet), was described in June 1881 as one of "the most thriving and prosperous mining camps of the San Juan." A business and social center for the upper Animas miners, its fate lay with that of nearby mines. They gave it moments of prosperity and a gentle decline into oblivion. Not even the coming of the railroad could reverse the outcome.

Beyond Animas Forks, experienced four-wheelers can cross Cinnamon or Engineer passes to Lake City, or continue northwest to Ouray. Spectacular scenery and a variety of mining sites and ruins await travelers on either route.

Back in Silverton, the left (west) fork of County Road 110 at the end of Greene Street takes you to another mining area. The road goes to Gladstone, platted in 1877, near the site of the current Sunnyside Mine operations. Growth came slowly here — only eighteen people were counted by the 1890 census taker, and Gladstone never grew beyond a small camp. The Gold King Mine, this district's major producer, outdid all of the other mines in San Juan County in 1902 with a production of 72,000 tons.

At one time, the Silverton, Gladstone and Northerly Railroad — yet another Mears enterprise — edged the banks of Cement Creek. Ore trucks now rumble down the road on their way to the mill on the Animas River. In its heyday, Gladstone had businesses, hotels, homes, mines, and mills. Nothing remains except some foundations.

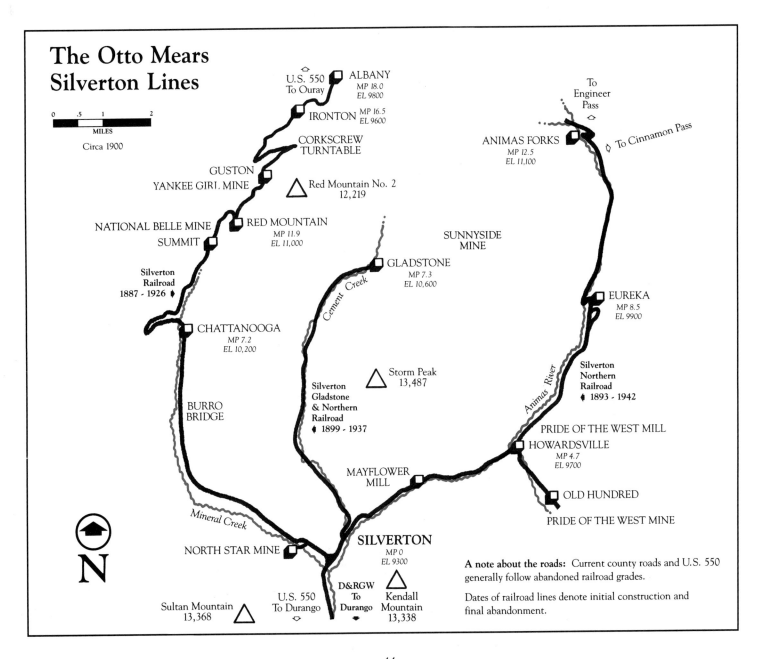

The Otto Mears
Silverton Lines

0   .5   1   2
MILES

Circa 1900

U.S. 550
To Ouray

ALBANY
MP 18.0
EL 9800

IRONTON
MP 16.5
EL 9600

CORKSCREW
TURNTABLE

GUSTON

YANKEE GIRL MINE

Red Mountain No. 2
12,219

NATIONAL BELLE MINE
SUMMIT

RED MOUNTAIN
MP 11.9
EL 11,000

Silverton
Railroad
1887 - 1926

GLADSTONE
MP 7.3
EL 10,600

SUNNYSIDE
MINE

To
Engineer
Pass

To Cinnamon Pass

ANIMAS FORKS
MP 12.5
EL 11,100

Cement Creek

EUREKA
MP 8.5
EL 9900

CHATTANOOGA
MP 7.2
EL 10,200

Storm Peak
13,487

Silverton
Gladstone
& Northern
Railroad
1899 - 1937

Animas River

Silverton
Northern
Railroad
1893 - 1942

BURRO
BRIDGE

PRIDE OF THE WEST MILL

HOWARDSVILLE
MP 4.7
EL 9700

MAYFLOWER
MILL

OLD HUNDRED

PRIDE OF THE WEST MINE

Mineral Creek

NORTH STAR MINE

SILVERTON
MP 0
EL 9300

Sultan Mountain
13,368

U.S. 550
To Durango

D&RGW
To
Durango

Kendall
Mountain
13,338

A note about the roads: Current county roads and U.S. 550 generally follow abandoned railroad grades.

Dates of railroad lines denote initial construction and final abandonment.

N

U.S. 550 north to Ouray follows the route of another Mears railroad, the Silverton, built in 1887 to tap the mines at Red Mountain. In the mid-1880s, no San Juan mining district glittered more alluringly than Red Mountain. The rush to it began in 1882 with the discovery and opening of the Yankee Girl and Guston mines. The Yankee Girl ore, yielding 2,000 ounces of silver per ton, generated immediate publicity and quickly brought investors. Late in the decade, English investors controlled the major mines. Ouray and Silverton fought to dominate this district, a prize worth gaining as silver production averaged over $800,000 a year for five years, at a time when the price per ounce hovered around one dollar.

Just before starting up Red Mountain Pass — called Sheridan Pass by nineteenth-century San Juaners — you can see the few remaining buildings of the little camp of Chattanooga. The highly urbanized Red Mountain district included the small settlements of Red Mountain City (Congress), Red Mountain, Guston, and Ironton. Ironton, at the southern end of Ironton Park, was the largest of the group with a peak population of over 300. It was also the most sheltered and the lowest in elevation (9,800 feet). A fire destroyed Red Mountain, "Sky City," in August 1892, and it never rebounded. All the old camps are ghost towns today.

Above: Otto Mears, the "Pathfinder of the San Juans," who built a transportation empire in southwest Colorado, first with toll roads, then with railroads. *Colorado Historical Society.*

Right: Engine and ticket office of the Silverton, Gladstone & Northerly railroad. This building also served as the assay office for the Gold King Mine. Note the bicycle and boardwalk. *San Juan Historical Society.*

The Guston Mine on Red Mountain near Silverton. Winter created huge problems for miners, even after the railroads arrived. *Gregory Collection.*

Underground at the Sunnyside Mine, one of Silverton's major producers, about 1902. *Allan Bird.*

Mules waiting in Silverton with rails for the mines. *Denver Public Library, Western History Department.*

Engine 473 parked at Silverton. *Colorado Historical Society.*

Acknowledgements

Many people over the years have provided the assistance, information, and encouragement that has made my research on Durango and the San Juans possible. On this project, I would especially like to thank Glen Crandall for his yeoman photographic work and, as always, my wife Gay for her continued editorial help.

For those who wish to continue research on the area, I recommend the Center of Southwest Studies at Fort Lewis College, the Durango Public Library, and the San Juan County Historical Society.

About the Author

Duane A. Smith is widely respected as one of the foremost authorities on the American mining frontier. A graduate of the University of Colorado and long-time professor of history at Fort Lewis College in Durango, Smith has authored and co-authored nineteen books and numerous articles, many of which focus on southwestern Colorado. His writings include *Rocky Mountain Mining Camps, Song of the Hammer and Drill: The Colorado San Juans, 1860-1914, Rocky Mountain Boom Town: A History of Durango, Colorado,* and a soon-to-be published history of Mesa Verde National Park. Not content with merely writing about his subject, Smith has spent many grand days exploring the West's rich past on four-wheel drive excursions and high country hikes.

Other Titles in the
Cordillera Press Historic Mining District Series

Guide to the Georgetown-Silver Plume Historic District
Guide to Historic Central City & Black Hawk
Guide to Historic Western Boulder County
Guide to Historic Aspen and the Roaring Fork Valley